Makayla's Great Discovery

Story by Judy Anderson
Illustrations by Hatice Bayramoglu
Editor Violetta Anderson

The night seemed to drag on and on for Makayla. She tossed and turned all throughout the night. Rolling from one end of the bed to the other. She tried fluffing her pillows, and still, found it hard to sleep. Makayla was filled with so much excitement, knowing that tomorrow would be the very first day of school, and the beginning of a brand new outlook on life. "I really need to sleep," said Makayla, checking her alarm clock for at least the fifth time. She'd awakened every hour on the hour, just to make sure her clock was set for the right time. Makayla thought about this day all summer and didn't realize how quickly the school year had actually arrived. She'd even gone to bed early so that she'd be well rested and on time for the first day of school. Unable to keep her eyes open any longer, she finally drifted off with her hand still clutching her alarm clock.

At last, morning finally arrived, and Makayla awakened with a smile that was beautiful and bright. Just like the sun that kissed her cheek to wake her before her alarm could even sound. Makayla's alarm sounded a ring that could wake the entire neighborhood. "This is going to be the best school year ever," said Makayla, climbing out of bed, sliding her feet into her slippers. After a good long stretch, she began jumping up and down. Up and down. Singing with joyous rhythm, "It's the first day of school, it's the first day of school, I can't wait, it's the first day of school." Makayla's mom could hear the sound of her jumping up and down as she prepared breakfast for the morning. Makayla's bedroom was right above the kitchen; therefore, her mom always knew when she'd awakened in the morning.

Hmmmmm, "What should I wear," thought Makayla as she searched through her school uniforms. She quickly decided that a school uniform just wasn't special enough to wear, not when discussing her great discovery. So she picked the prettiest dress in her closet and quickly dressed for school. Before leaving her bedroom, she turned to look at herself in the mirror, just one last time. She giggled and smiled. Makayla saw an image in that mirror that was quite different from how she viewed herself in the past, and what she discovered played a vital role in her rise to love and accept who she is. She was now ready for the first day of school and all the happier.

Skipping through her bedroom door, and yelling loudly down the stairs to her mom. Makayla asked, "Is breakfast ready yet?" Makayla's mom answered, "Yes, breakfast is ready, you can come down now." "We wouldn't want you to be late for school, you've only talked about this day the entire summer." "Yes mother," with excitement in her voice, "I'll be down in a second." "Good morning mommy," said Makayla. "Good morning daddy," kissing them both on the cheek. "It's a beautiful day, isn't it?" "Yes, Makayla, it's a beautiful day." "Now eat your breakfast before it gets cold," said Makayla's mom. "Yes mother," replied Makayla, as she grabbed a piece of buttered toast, gulped down a glass of freshly squeezed orange juice and within minutes, she was finished with her breakfast. "Slow down Makayla, you'll get to school soon enough," said her mom.

But Makayla couldn't wait to get to school to tell her closest friends what she'd discovered over her summer vacation. Makayla's friends had all gone away for the summer leaving her behind. She didn't get a chance to tell them of her great discovery, and today would be the big day. Finally, Makayla arrived at school and found all of her friends, Briana, Aaliyah, Dawnisha, Anaiah, and Hollie, standing around the playground, gossiping about all the exciting events that took place over summer vacation. Amusement parks and splash parks seemed to have made everyone's list. This made some of the children feel as though their summer excitement didn't compare much, not when it came to amusement parks. As far as Makayla's friends were concerned, there wasn't anything that could compete with splash parks and amusement parks.

Makayla didn't seem to mind that she hadn't actually gone anywhere for summer vacation, she figured that she may not have visited an amusement park or traveled out of the city, but what she discovered would be worth more than gold in her book. It would be worth more than 10 amusement parks put together as far as she was concerned. There wasn't a splash park around that could compare to what she discovered from her granddad's visit. Makayla listened with great anticipation of telling everyone what she'd discovered over the summer and just needed to hear that one familiar sound, "The school bell." It would be the best sound Makayla's heard all morning. And there it was, the sound of the bell. Makayla could now enter her classroom and take her seat. She sat right in front of the class where everyone could hear what she had to say. Makayla knew that every year after summer vacation, the teachers would ask the same famous question, "What was your summer vacation like." She was more than prepared to answer. Makayla sat her book carry-on close to her desk. She sat up nice and tall in preparation of hearing her teacher say those magic words, summer vacation.

Math

How to Divide

59
7⟌413
35
63
63
0

How to Multiply

23
x 82
46
184
1,886

A good book is a good friend!

Makayla sat patiently, thinking to herself, "I've prepared for this day during my entire summer vacation, i've practiced over and over again. Pacing back and forth, looking at myself in mirrors. I've watched my words form as I said them aloud." "I'm hoping that I won't forget all that my granddad taught me over the summer. Nawww, I'm sure I'll do just fine. An unfamiliar voice coming from the front of the class caught Makayla's attention. A tall, slender, women with glasses hanging from the tip of her nose, a skirt that was so long that it nearly touched the floor, a tightly wrapped bun in the back of her hair said, "Good morning class! My name is Mrs. Dixon, and I'll be your fifth-grade teacher this year. I hope that you all had a fantastic vacation." "I can't wait to hear all about it. In the meantime, I've planned lots of exciting events for you this school year." "We will go into great detail about what is expected from you as students of fifth grade. Welcome to Sojourner Truth Elementary School!"

"I'd first like to go over the first assignment for the morning, it involves drawing a picture of what your vacation was like." "Be creative, the goal is to describe in pictures what you would have said to me in words. So let's begin class. Remember to have lots and lots of fun with it. Makayla looked as if she'd seen a ghost." She thought for a second, and with great disappointment, "I've practiced all summer long about what I'm going to say, and how I'm going to say it, and now the teacher decides to do something different this year." "I can't believe it! I'm ruined. What am I going to do? How can I explain to the class what I've discovered in a silly picture? That's it, it's over." "I should have known that something like this would happen." "Looks as if someone should've taken art lessons over the summer," thought Makayla. Maybe I could draw a picture of the photos granddad showed me.

All of a sudden, before even completing her thought, an outburst from Makayla, excitedly shouting, "I got it, I got it!" The entire class turned and focused their attention on Makayla's outburst, they all wondered, "What in sands land has gotten into her." Her friends all thought that she'd been acting mighty strange lately; compared to the last time they'd seen her. They couldn't quite put their finger on it, but they'd soon find out just what it was that had Makayla extremely happy.

Math

A good book 📚 is a good friend!

How to Divide

59
7)413
35
63
63
0

How to Multiply

Makayla grabbed her construction paper, crayons, and pencil. She attempted to put those thoughts onto paper. "Now, where should I begin? I've already ruined two sheets of construction paper." "The idea was so clear to me a moment ago, now I can't think of what I was going to draw," said Makayla. "Should I draw the pictures that granddad showed me? No, it may be a little difficult trying to draw the photos. I know! I could cut my granddads photos and paste them on the construction paper." "Nope, can't do that either, my granddad wouldn't want me to cut up his photos. He treasures them, and they mean the world to him." "He said that they were the link to my future. Hmmmmm this is really going to be a disaster, I can already see it," thought Makayla. "I didn't know that I would be in a painting class today. This is not what I had in mind, but I guess it's not so bad after all." My mother always said that, "I have a special talent." She said that, "I have the power to do whatever I want to. That I should always aim higher." I believe her! So here it goes.

As soon as Makayla prepared to start her drawing, she noticed that there was a crayon missing. She frantically searched, and yes, it was missing from her box. "Oh no!!!! Where is it? I can't find it anywhere." She desperately searched; emptying out the entire box of crayons and still, it was missing. She scooted her chair back to look under her desk, no crayon. She checked inside of her desk repeatedly. Over and over again, she searched the same area. Still, the crayon was missing. Makayla unintentionally blurts out to get her teacher's attention. "Mrs. Dixon! Mrs. Dixon, the brown crayon is missing. I can't find it anywhere. Please, say you have another. Without it, I won't be able to start my drawing. I really want to share with the class what I've discovered over the summer."

Ideas
Voice
Word
9 Good Habids for all readers
While I read
MAK-AYLA

"Well Makayla, I'm sure you'll find another. Can you replace it with another color?" Makayla's eyes grew extremely large as she thought to herself, "Another color, no other color will do! I just have to have brown." "This is not good, not good at all." Just when Makayla thought that she'd never complete the entire drawing, her friend Anaiah, walked over to Makayla's desk, and said to her, "Here Makayla, you can use mine, I didn't need it anyway. Now you'll be able to finish your drawing." Makayla's smile lit up the room. She realized what her friend had done. Anaiah unselfishly allowed Makayla to have the crayon from her very own box. "Thanks Anaiah, you're the best," said Makayla.

A relieved Makayla continued to focus on how she would put her discovery down on paper. She began to think of her granddad's visit over the summer. He shared many, many, stories with Makayla. Her granddad read to her every single day during summer vacation. He brought with him a gift that would change Makayla's life forever. "This may not be such a terrible idea after all," thought Makayla. "Now everyone will get to see exactly what I'm explaining to them. Before the assignment, the class would have only heard about what I've learned over my vacation, now they will get to see and hear." "My words and a picture. I think it will work. "I'll just focus on the books my granddad read to me and photos that he showed me. I can even do a collage and that way, it won't be so difficult to draw." "I'll give it my best, and I guess I'll be ok. Just remember granddad's voice."

Makayla's granddad spent the entire summer with her and read to her often because he knew that his grand-baby was being mistreated by some of the children at school. They teased her all the time, calling her mean names like, "black girl, and tar girl." Her granddad knew all about it. He wanted his granddaughter to be proud of who she was. But Makayla had trouble accepting the complexion of her skin. She never looked at herself as being really dark. But the other children did, and they were just a little bit lighter than she was, so she really didn't understand what the problem was. It made her hate the complexion of her skin. It really hurt Makayla's feelings. It changed the way she felt about school and she began to make up excuses by telling her mom that she didn't feel well. Her love for school vanished. She searched magazine after magazine, hoping to find someone who looked just like her. Makayla was never able to find those photos and it was beginning to look as if nothing would make her except that she truly is, a beautiful little princess. Every photo that she saw was of someone who didn't look anything like her, and that certainly bothered her. "Am I not pretty?" thought Makayla.

Makayla's granddad loved her more than anything in the world and didn't like that she was struggling with such a serious issue of accepting who she was. He always told Makayla to remain true to herself and to love herself first, no matter how anyone else felt about her. "Never look to the world to tell you what beauty is," said Makayla's granddad. "True Beauty lies within oneself," and Makayla would hear this from him the entire summer. He was determined to let his grandbaby know about her greatness. Makayla wanted to take all she'd learned from her granddad and scream it out to the whole world. Therefore; this project was especially important to Makayla, she just had to let everyone know what she discovered, and so she did.

Makayla began drawing images of beautiful queens and kings adorned in beautiful garments. They wore beautiful jewels and sat on large thrones. She drew giant pyramids and wondered how the people were able to climb so high. She drew beautiful ceremonies with people dancing in laughter. Everyone seemed to be really happy. Makayla remembered her granddad telling her that, "Her ancestors were the first creators of medicine, mathematics, and science. You name it! We did it! Most importantly, he said that, "The ancient Egyptians were actually of African descent." As her granddad continued to speak, Makayla felt a strong sense of pride. She saw pictures of beautiful green trees. She saw beautiful sand with glistening speckles in them. She told her granddad, "I've never seen anything like this in all of my life, not in any of my school books."

While patiently waiting to hear Mrs. Dixon say those famous words, "Present your drawing." Makayla continued to reflect on the wonderful stories of her granddad's early travels. He showed her the most beautiful photos she'd ever seen. What excited her most was that the photos shown to her were photos of her ancestors whose skin was just like hers. Dark skin, that glistened like gold. Finally, she'd found someone just like her, and they were of great importance to her history and future. Not only were they of royalty, but intelligent, peaceful, and happy. They loved, and embraced the beauty of their skin, something Makayla had now decided to do. The Ancient Egyptians lived their lives in peace and harmony. It was a time of celebration. There wasn't any crime! There wasn't any sickness! My granddad said that my ancestors had the ability to heal themselves if they got sick. They used plants and foods from the earth to heal any sickness they wanted to. They even made their own gold. He also said that, "The women in the land held powerful positions." He told Makayla that the men in the Nile Valley listened carefully to the queens of the land and got advice from them.

The moment Makayla's waited for. Those words she'd long
to hear, "Everyone put your crayons away and get ready to
showcase your talent,:" said Mrs. Dixon. "I am sure you
all did a fantastic job, can't wait to see. Who'd like to
present their drawing first?" Makayla's hand flew up in
the air, swaying her desk from side to side, her hand
swinging radically causing her pencil to land way across the
room near Dawnisha's seat. "Pick me," thought Makayla.
This is what she'd waited for. This is what she'd practiced
the entire summer for. "At last, the day has come," thought
Makayla. "Me! Me! Me!" Swaying her hand from side to
side. "Mrs. Dixon, I'd like to go first."

"Alright, Makayla, will you come to the front of the class," said Mrs. Dixon. "Yes Mrs. Dixon," said Makayla, as she approached the front of the class. Grinning from ear to ear while taping her drawing to the chalkboard. Makayla anxiously explained to her classmates what she'd drawn, and the whole class burst into laughter. Pointing at Makayla's drawing. Makayla grew confused and wasn't smiling anymore. She didn't understand why they all laughed at her drawing. She thought that her drawing was absolutely beautiful. She didn't know why her classmates didn't like it. Makayla worked so hard on her masterpiece, and with great pride. She'd carefully thought of every word her granddad told her. Makayla stood there with her head hung low in embarrassment. She just knew that they'd all like her drawing. "What could have gone wrong," thought Makayla. Her classmate Andre blurted out, "You messed up Makayla. Egyptians weren't that dark; they had light, light skin. Like in all of the movies and books."

Mrs. Dixon yells loudly, "Enough I say! Stop it right now! It's not polite to laugh and point at someone else. I'm surprised at your behavior." "I'm sure Makayla didn't mean to color them brown, she knows that the Egyptians weren't brown." Makayla turned and looked at her teacher with sheer disappointment. Of all people, Makayla certainly expected her teacher to believe her. She honestly couldn't imagine her teacher not believing her. Makayla turned to her teacher with the surest of confidence and said, "Mrs. Dixon I did mean to color them brown. I purposely colored them, brown. That is why I searched for the brown crayon. I just had to have brown." Makayla asked Mrs. Dixon if she could share a little secret with Andre. Mrs. Dixon agreed. She gave Makayla permission to continue. Makayla turned to Andre and said, "I'd like to share what my grandfather has already proven to me. We call them Egyptians, but granddad said that before they were called Egyptians, they were called Kamites." "Egypt was the name given to the land after several invasions. Egypt used to be called Kemet, and it's located in Africa." "Did you know that Kemet means, the land of blacks?"

"I have proof! I have the photos that my granddad gave me to show the class," said Makayla. She pulled the photos from her carry-on that were given to her by her granddad. The photos were taken in Egypt. Proving her discovery to be indeed true. Makayla's classmates all gathered around her photos to get a better look. They've never seen photos like that before in any of their schoolbooks. They were certainly the most beautiful photos of brown skin and dark skin kings and queens. All different shades of brown, "just like a rainbow," said one of Makayla's classmates. "They're beautiful," said Makayla's friend Briana, as she passed around Makayla's photos for viewing. The children were so excited about what they were seeing; they didn't realize that they were pushing one another to get to those photos. "I never knew that our ancestors were of royalty Makayla. I apologize for laughing, but I honestly didn't know," said Andre. "It's Ok Andre," said Makayla. "I didn't know either, but I sure am happy granddad knew! Names can't hurt me anymore because; I now know who I am. I am from greatness. I am that I am."

"This is great Makayla! I've learned a very valuable lesson today myself," said Mrs. Dixon. "I am delighted that your granddad has shared with you a piece of our great history." "I am really eager to learn more. I have an idea class; let's see the hands of students who want to continue this venture as a field trip." "Me, Me! I want to go. So would I," yelled Makayla's classmates. "This is great," said Mrs. Dixon. "I've never seen my students so eager to learn. Let's dedicate ourselves to researching who it is we really are." "Hopefully we can ask Makayla's granddad to join us as a tour guide. What do you think about that class?" "Yayyyyyy! Shouted Makayla's classmates. "We're going to the museum, to see for ourselves. We're going to the museum, to see for ourselves." "We're going to the museum to see for ourselves, thanks to Makayla, we'll see for ourselves." Makayla's classmates never knew about the past that was so tightly kept secret from them.

THE END

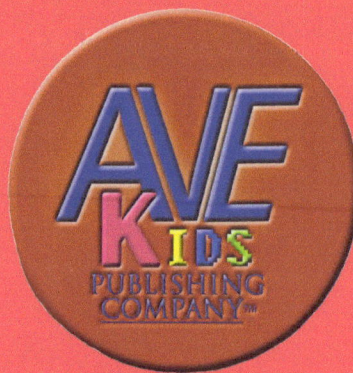

www.avekidspublishing.com

www.ingramcontent.com/pod-product-compliance
Lightning Source LLC
LaVergne TN
LVHW072053070426
835508LV00002B/82